Bug Business

Ann Weil

STECK-VAUGHN
ELEMENTARY · SECONDARY · ADULT · LIBRARY

A Harcourt Company

www.steck-vaughn.com

Photography: p.iv ©Kazuyoshi Nomachi/Photo Researchers, Inc.; p.2 ©D. Cavagnaro/Visuals Unlimited, Inc.; p.6 ©Steve Callahan/Visuals Unlimited, Inc.; p.7 ©Bill Beatty/Visuals Unlimited, Inc.; p.8 ©Tim Williams; pp.15–16 ©Mary McAdam; p.17 ©Scott Camazine/Photo Researchers, Inc.; pp.21–22 ©Bill Ballard; pp.28–29 ©Tom McHugh/Photo Researchers, Inc.; p.30 ©Alvin Simmons; p.32 ©Shane Keyser; p.35 ©Frank Lane Picture Agency/CORBIS; p.36 ©Alison Wright/CORBIS; p.38 ©Macduff Everton/CORBIS.

Additional photography by Comstock, Inc., CORBIS, MetaTools, PhotoDisc, Inc.

ISBN 0-7398-5138-1

Contents

Chapter 1

Bugs Everywhere

"Get that thing off of me!" A lot of people get upset because of a crawling bug. Most insects don't harm us, though.

Insects Everywhere!

Nobody knows exactly how many different types of insects there are in the world. New **species** are still being discovered. A species is a group of plants or animals that have certain features in common. Scientists think there could be between five million and eighty million species of insects. For every person on Earth, there are more than one billion insects. That's a lot of insects!

Would this swarm of bugs make you nervous?

Insects come in all shapes, sizes, and colors. Some insects, like butterflies, are very colorful. Many butterflies have beautiful patterns on their wings. This makes them among the best-loved animals in the world.

Some insects are so tiny that you can't even see them. Others have shapes and colors that match the things around them. Some even look like small leaves and sticks. This makes it harder for other animals to find them.

The insects shown here, called walking sticks, look like twigs.

Leaf cutter ants can carry heavy loads.

Some insects are very strong. Ants can carry thirty times their own body weight. If you could lift thirty times your body weight, you might be able to pick up a car!

Insects can live in almost every kind of **environment**. Some of them can live in places that are too hot or too cold for people. A few insects can even live underwater.

Helpful Bugs and Pest Bugs

Some insects damage crops. This costs farmers a lot of money. Other insects feed on those pests. These helpful bugs can save farmers' crops from being destroyed by the pest bugs.

3

Other helpful bugs make our life sweeter. Bees make honey from **nectar** they gather from flowers. Some insects even help make our clothes. Have you ever touched real silk? Clothes made from silk look and feel soft. The thread used to make silk comes from **silkworms**. A silkworm is a type of caterpillar that makes fine threads of silk to build its cocoon. Inside their cocoons, these caterpillars grow into moths.

Many animals that we use for food eat insects. Some animals eat the animals that eat insects. So, in one way or another, many types of animals depend on insects.

Insects' bodies are very different from ours. They have three pairs of jointed legs. Most insects also have wings. Insect bodies have three sections. The first is the head. The head includes the insect's mouth, eyes, and antennae. The second is the **thorax**. This is where the insect's legs attach to its body. If the insect has wings, these also attach to the thorax. The third part is the insect's **abdomen**. It includes the stomach.

What Is an Insect?

All insects have four things in common:

1 An insect has three pairs of jointed legs.

2 An insect's body has three major parts.

3 An insect has a skeleton on the outside of its body.

4 An insect develops from an egg.

antennae

head

thorax

abdomen

Growth and Change

Your skin and bones grow as you do. An insect does not have skin or bones. It has a hard shell on the outside of its body. As the insect grows larger, a new shell forms underneath the old one. Then the old shell pops open, and the insect crawls out. This is called **molting**.

Most insects change form at least once during their life. This process is called **metamorphosis**. Through metamorphosis, some insects grow wings. A squirmy caterpillar can even become a delicate butterfly.

This insect is in the final stages of molting.

This spider has caught two beetles in its web.

Are Spiders Bugs?

Many people think spiders are insects. Spiders and insects belong to the same large group of animals. Spiders are not insects, though. A spider has eight legs, and its body has only two parts. The head and thorax are joined together into one part. The abdomen is another part. These two parts are joined by a thin waist.

All spiders are **predators**. Their favorite meal is insects. Altogether, spiders can eat as many as 200 **trillion** insects each year. With an appetite like that, it's amazing that there are any insects left on the planet!

Chapter 2

Tim Williams
Bug Wrangler

Lights...Camera...Action...BUGS!

Have you seen a movie or TV show that featured cockroaches, ants, or other bugs? Did you ever wonder how these tiny actors learned their parts? That's the work of Tim Williams.

Tim is a professional bug **wrangler**. He works behind the scenes to make sure the animals play their parts in front of the camera. Tim has handled insects and spiders for Hollywood movies.

Bugs don't give Tim Williams the creeps.

Tarantulas on TV

Tim's first job working with **tarantulas** was for a battery commercial. Tarantulas are a type of spider. They look scary, even to a professional bug wrangler. Although a tarantula bite usually won't kill a person, it can hurt a lot. "I wasn't comfortable with the tarantulas at first," Tim says.

In the battery commercial, a couple's old car is broken down in the desert. It's supposed to be very hot outside. The only way for the couple to stay cool is with a small, battery-operated fan. The director of the commercial wanted a tarantula to walk around near the car. He thought this would make people think the place was hot and deserted.

Only one tarantula was needed on camera. Tim had two tarantulas with him. That way, one could rest while the other was "working."

Tim thinks handling bugs is the easy part. Sometimes it's much harder working with the human actors. The actors in this battery commercial didn't have to touch the tarantulas. Still, they were **apprehensive**.

Scorpions, Tarantulas, and TV Stars

A few years later, Tim handled tarantulas and **scorpions** for a TV talk show. Scorpions are related to spiders. They are not insects. A scorpion can sting a person with the tip of its tail. Most of the time, a scorpion's sting won't kill a person, but it is very painful.

At first, the show's two stars wouldn't even come into the room with the animals. "They were completely terrified," Tim says. Tim was worried, too, but for a different reason. He was worried for the safety of the animals. If the people were scared, they might drop an animal. That could hurt or even kill it.

"The best way to keep people comfortable is to educate them," Tim explains. "I teach people to let the spider think it's just walking on a surface. That surface may be your hand, but the tarantula won't know it's being held."

On the talk show, Tim was calm and relaxed. Soon the stars were handling the tarantulas on camera. One even wore a tarantula on her head!

Secrets of a Bug Wrangler

Tim has trained many different types of wild and **domestic** animals. Bugs are different, though. "You can't really train a bug," Tim says. Besides, Tim rarely meets his insect or spider actors until the morning of the shoot.

The director tells Tim what he wants the bugs or spiders to do for the camera. Tim uses the animals' own instincts to get them to do what the director wants.

"Spiders would rather climb up than down," Tim explains. "To get a scene with the spider climbing up is easy. Climbing down is hard." When a scene calls for a spider to move down, Tim ties a piece of very thin fishing line around the spider's body. Then he stands on a ladder and slowly lowers the line and the spider.

Tim knows how to get a bug or spider to move in a certain direction. He blows through a straw so the air hits the animal in the back, and the animal walks away. Tim can get the animal to move faster by blowing harder.

"Bugs and spiders move faster when they're warm," Tim explains. Tim sometimes points a warm hair dryer at the animals to get them to move faster on camera.

Bug Safety

An important part of Tim's job is to keep the animals safe. Whenever animals are used in movies or on TV, an official watches to make sure they are not harmed. Tim has a perfect record. "I've never lost a bug!"

Chapter 3

Mary McAdam
Beekeeper

Mary McAdam started keeping bees a few years ago. She learned how to keep bees from her uncle. A beekeeper is someone who keeps hives of bees. The bees produce honey and wax for candles. Mary now has eight hives. Four are at her home in Nine Mile Falls, Washington. Four others are spread through her community.

Some people asked Mary to put her hives on their property to help **pollinate** their apple orchards. As bees fly from apple blossom to apple blossom, tiny hairs on their bodies pick up pollen and carry it to another tree. This helps the trees produce fruit.

Mary McAdam's bees are making honey.

Mary even started a **Web site** about beekeeping. She wanted to show others that beekeeping is a fun hobby and a great thing for a family to do together. 🐝

Mary's bees have become a family project. Her 11-year-old son, Wesley, is already an experienced beekeeper. Mary's two other sons also help out. So does Wesley's cousin Jerod.

Mary says Wesley is the only one who can fit into her uncle's old bee suit. "My uncle was rather small, so Wesley wears it while I take my chances."

Wesley holds a special beekeeper's tool called a **smoker** next to one of the hives. Beekeepers use smoke to relax the bees and keep them from stinging. When the bees smell smoke, they go into the hive and gulp honey. Then, just like a family after Thanksgiving dinner, the bees settle down for a nap after their big meal. Then the beekeeper can work in the hive with less risk of getting stung.

Wesley McAdam uses the smoker.

Worker bees surround their queen.

The queen bee is larger than the other bees. She lays all the eggs for her colony. There is usually only one queen in each hive.

The workers are the female children of the queen. Workers do not lay eggs and do not mate. They have many different jobs, including scouting for nectar, which is used to make honey.

The **drones** are the male children of the queen. Their only job is to mate with a queen. They usually mate with queens of other hives. Drones depend on workers to feed them. In the fall, food becomes scarce, and the drones die.

It's a Swarm!

Bees swarm when it's time for some of them to leave and start a new hive. Usually this happens when a new queen is born inside the hive. Then the older queen may leave the hive along with many of her children.

When a swarm of bees leaves the hive, it often clusters around a tree branch. Some of the worker bees leave the swarm to scout out new places for the colony to live. Then the bees travel together to make a new hive.

Beekeepers can capture the swarm and put the bees in a new hive. Mary remembers the first time she did this.

"One of the teachers I work with requested that I put a hive at his orchard. One day he called to tell me that the bees were swarming. I got the swarm (my first!) and put the bees in a new box. They have been doing well ever since."

Bee Stings

The first time Mary got stung, it was just above her eye. That part of her face swelled up a little, but it was the itching that really annoyed her.

"The last time I was stung was on the lip." Now Mary wears a veil when she works with her bees. "It offers some protection. I can deal with stings on all exposed body parts except my face."

This swarm of bees clusters on a tree branch before starting a new colony.

Antonio Guillen
BugCamp Assistant

Antonio Guillen is only 17 years old, but he already knows more about insects than most adults know. He spent a summer working at BugCamp. His job was to help the staff run the camp.

How BugCamp Began

BugCamp got its start when Zeus Preckwinkle, a science teacher, made **arrangements** for a class visitor. He asked Dr. Bill Ballard to speak to his students. Dr. Ballard was the head of the insect department at Chicago's Field Museum.

Dr. Ballard told the class about his job at the Field Museum. One student asked how many people worked there. Dr. Ballard explained that there were about forty **curators**. He said there were also many people who volunteered. Some students asked if they could volunteer. Dr. Ballard told them they could.

That was how BugCamp began. The students helped the curators with their work. They learned a lot about insects at the same time. Now BugCamp is a ten-week summer program.

Antonio Goes to BugCamp

Antonio first became interested in insects in the eighth grade. He was in Zeus Preckwinkle's science class that year. Mr. Preckwinkle introduced the class to **entomology**. Entomology is the study of insects. Mr. Preckwinkle told the class that he was running a camp at the nearby Field Museum in Chicago. He explained that it would be a fun way for students to learn more about insects. Antonio applied, and he attended BugCamp during the summer of 1998.

Zeus Preckwinkle uses a net to collect insects at BugCamp.

Students help with important duties at BugCamp.

Antonio's BugCamp Experience

Antonio was 14 years old when he went to BugCamp in 1998. The students spent a lot of time at a nearby park called Ryerson Woods. They collected insects from the grass, soil, and air in this

550-acre park. Their work was used in an official report on the kinds of insect life at the park.

It was hard work collecting the insects, especially on very hot days. Antonio still thought the whole experience was a lot of fun. He liked being part of a team working on a **meaningful** project. He felt that he was helping to do something important.

BugCamp changed the way Antonio looked at nature. Before BugCamp, he saw insects only as pests. After that summer, he knew that insects weren't just pests. He learned the important role insects play on Earth.

On the Job

Three years later, Antonio was back collecting insects at BugCamp. This time he was a teacher's assistant. "It was during these field trips that I was able to help the most. I was able to show the kids where all the cool bugs were and how to catch them."

Antonio helped the BugCampers collect all sorts of insects. On one trip, they tried to get a lot of butterflies. On another, they collected mostly smaller insects. Once in a while, they would collect spiders.

Antonio had other duties, such as ordering equipment and making copies. He thought it was a great summer job. "It didn't even feel like a job. It just felt like being with friends, learning about stuff we're interested in."

Is a career with insects in Antonio's future? "I don't think I will get into the field of entomology when I grow up. I'm more interested in computer science and programming. Maybe someday I will find the perfect job where I can do what I love with insects and computers."

Chapter 5

Dr. Alvin Simmons
Researcher of Entomology

Dr. Alvin Simmons is a **Researcher** of Entomology. He develops new ways of controlling insect pests without using chemical **pesticides**. Dr. Simmons studies insects that damage crops. He identifies helpful bugs that feed on these insect pests. Using helpful bugs to control pest bugs and protect crops is called **biocontrol**.

Using fewer pesticides is safer for us and for the environment. Pesticides often kill helpful bugs along with pests. Dr. Simmons found that many helpful bugs can still live when farmers use only a small amount of pesticide.

Dr. Simmons studies both helpful bugs and pest bugs. One of the pests Dr. Simmons works to control is a type of insect called a **whitefly**. Whiteflies do a lot of damage to vegetable plants. Fortunately, some small, helpful wasps eat whiteflies. Farmers can buy these wasps and release them in their fields to protect their vegetable crops from whiteflies.

Ladybugs are one type of helpful insect.

Dr. Simmons uses biocontrol with his own plants. He releases ladybugs in his **greenhouse** to protect his plants. He says that the ladybugs eat many different types of pest bugs.

Growing Up with Bugs

Alvin Simmons's interest in bugs began when he was a child on his family's farm in North Carolina. When he worked on the farm, he saw many helpful insects and pest insects. He quickly learned that not all bugs are bad.

"There were many different types of ladybugs on the shrubs in our yard," he explains. "They were very colorful. I watched them feed on the pest insects."

Alvin Simmons understood the idea of biocontrol long before he'd heard that term. "On our farm, we used very little pesticides. That was good because there was no harm to the helpful bugs. The helpful bugs protected the crops."

Like many children, Simmons had a hands-on relationship with bugs from an early age. Some of his early experiments were with ants. "I put dirt over ant hills to see what happened. And I poured water across the ant trail to see if they would still travel in the same direction." ⚡

Keep Those Flies off My Cow!

Alvin noticed that **horseflies** were biting and bothering the cows on the farm. "To me, the cows were like large pets," he says. "Our favorite cow was named Betsy." He also noticed another insect that fed on the big horseflies. It looked like a hornet, but it did not sting people. "It was so satisfying to see them flying around Betsy and grabbing the biting flies. I was never afraid of them. I saw that they went for the flies and did not bother the cow or chase me."

Army ants march in a column along their trail.

As a child, he wished there were more of these helpful insects so that life for the cows would be easier. Later, he learned that this type of wasp is called a horse guard because it attacks and eats horseflies. Alvin thought that horse guards should be called "cow guards."

More Helpful Bugs

Some wasps sting people, but others are helpful. Alvin noticed a type of wasp that fed on insects that were eating the vegetables growing on the farm. These tiny wasps didn't bother people.

Alvin Simmons is shown here instructing a student.

"I found that there are more of these good wasps on some types of plants than on others." He is now looking at new ways of planting crops to increase the number of helpful bugs. More helpful bugs means fewer pest bugs and less crop damage. This is good news for farmers.

Food for Thought

Dr. Simmons likes his job. He likes working with insects and plants. His work helps farmers produce more crops. Finding ways to control pests without pesticides helps protect the environment from pollution, too. It also results in foods that are safer to eat. That's a lot to think about next time you bite into a vegetable. ⚡

Chapter 6

Dr. Mike Smith
Professor of Entomology

Mike Smith grew up in Oklahoma. He visited his grandparents and his great-grandmother during the summers. "They all had big vegetable gardens and fruit orchards," he says. "I spent lots of time catching bugs."

Mike is part Cherokee. Being American Indian gave him a different view of insects. He explains that insects are important in Cherokee stories. He says the spider is **revered** because it helped build the **Sacred** Fire of the Cherokee. The water bug also plays an important part in the Cherokee creation story.

Now Mike is an **entomologist** at Kansas State University. He also teaches younger students about insects. He developed a course for children called "Fun with Bugs." Mike uses the Madagascar hissing cockroach in his Fun with Bugs class. "They hold up to rough handling from the kids," Mike explains.

At first some of the children were **wary** of these big, noisy bugs. After a few of the braver children let the bugs crawl on them, everyone wanted a turn. Mike says that teachers have even requested hissing cockroaches as classroom pets.

Mike Smith doesn't mind bugs at all.

Chapter 7

Magdalena Gonzalez
Wool Dyer

Cochineal insects are tiny bugs that feed on the prickly pear cactus. Some people consider them pests because they can destroy big, beautiful cactus plants. These insects also are used to make a natural red coloring called cochineal dye.

Cochineal dye is used to color wool for rugs and other woven products. It also is used in some foods and **cosmetics**. Cochineal dye is safe and natural. Some red dyes made from chemicals are not safe to eat. Many countries have **banned** the use of these dangerous dyes.

In the past, Mexico produced most of the cochineal dye used in the world. That was before chemical dyes became popular. Most of the world's cochineal dye now comes from Chile, Peru, and the Canary Islands. There are still a few places in Mexico that raise cochineal insects as they did hundreds of years ago. The bugs are collected off the cactuses. Some Mexican weavers buy the cochineal insects to make their own dye. They use the dye to color their wool before weaving it into cloth. ⚡

Cochineal beetles hide under clusters of white fluff on this prickly pear cactus pad.

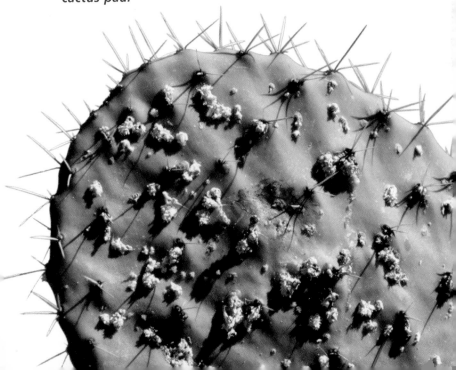

Cochineal Farmer: Juan Aquilino

Juan Aquilino lives in a village in Mexico. He learned all about cochineal farming from his father. He has about two acres of prickly pear cactuses. The cochineal insects live on these cactuses. Juan sells most of his cochineal bugs to the weavers in a nearby village.

Wool Dyer: Magdalena Gonzalez

The nearby village is a very **traditional** place. Life there is a lot like it was hundreds of years ago. Its people have woven wool rugs and saddle blankets in the same way for generations.

Magdalena Gonzalez buys the cochineal bugs from Juan Aquilino or another cochineal farmer. Cochineal dye is sold by weight. It takes more than 100,000 bugs to make a pound of dye.

Magdalena puts the dye into boiling water and adds the wool. The wool sits in the water for about an hour. The longer the wool is left in the hot water, the darker the color becomes.

A man grinds red powder to make dye in a traditional manner.

Plain cochineal dye will color wool a deep, dark red. Magdalena can add other ingredients to the dye to change the color. Adding lemon or orange juice turns the color more orange-red. Adding baking soda or ash turns the color more purple and blue.

Rug Weaver: Ruben Gonzalez

Magdalena's father, Ruben Gonzalez, learned weaving from his father. He has been a weaver all

A woman examines bottles of red dye.

his life. Now his wife Elena and their five grown children work together in the family business. After Magdalena dyes the wool, family members weave it into rugs.

Traditional Work in Modern Times

Juan Aquilino and Magdalena Gonzalez and her family work much as their ancestors did before them. However, cochineal dye is very expensive compared to chemical dyes. Many Mexican weavers cannot afford cochineal dye. It is easier and less expensive to buy ready-made products. It may be only a matter of time before cochineal insects are no longer part of the weaving tradition.

Insects and Us

Providing cochineal dye is one of many ways insects help people. Next time you put honey on a piece of toast or eat an apple, you might think about the bees that made the honey and pollinated the apple trees. The next time you feel a bug crawling on your arm, you might think twice before brushing it away. ⚡

Glossary

abdomen (AB duh muhn) *noun* The abdomen is the part of an animal's body that contains its stomach.

apprehensive (ap ree HEHN sihv) *adjective* Apprehensive means nervous or afraid.

arrangements (uh RAYNJ muhnts) *noun* Arrangements are plans.

banned (BAND) *verb* Banned means did not allow.

biocontrol (BY oh kuhn trohl) *noun* Biocontrol is a way of using one kind of living thing to keep another kind of living thing under control.

cochineal (KAHCH uh neel) *adjective* Cochineal insects are used to make a red dye, which is also called cochineal.

cosmetics (kahz MEHT ihks) *noun* Cosmetics are creams or powders worn on the face to make it more beautiful.

curators (KYOO rayt uhrz) *noun* Curators are people in charge of part of a museum or zoo.

domestic (doh MEHS tihk) *adjective* Domestic means tame.

drones (DROHNZ) *noun* Drones are male bees. Drones do not sting people or help make honey.

entomologist (ehn tuh MAHL uh jihst) *noun* An entomologist is a person who studies insects.

entomology (ehn tuh MAHL uh jee) *noun* Entomology is the study of insects.

environment (ehn VY ruhn muhnt) *noun* Environment is the place and the conditions in which an animal lives.

greenhouse (GREEN hows) *noun* A greenhouse is a type of building used for growing plants. It has a clear plastic or glass roof and sides that let in the sunshine and keep the plants warm.

horseflies (HAWRS flyz) *noun* Horseflies are large flies that bite horses, cattle, and people.

meaningful (MEE nihng fuhl) *adjective* Something that is meaningful has an important purpose.

metamorphosis (meht uh MAWR fuh sihs) *noun* Metamorphosis is a process that some insects go through when they change form.

molting (MOHLT ihng) *noun* Molting is a process by which an animal sheds its body's outer covering.

nectar (NEHK tuhr) *noun* Nectar is a sweet liquid found inside many flowers.

pesticides (PEHS tuh sydz) *noun* Pesticides are chemical poisons used to kill harmful insects.

pollinate (PAHL uh nayt) *verb* Pollinate means carry pollen from one part of a flower to another. Many plants and trees must be pollinated in order to bear fruit.

predators (PREHD uh tuhrz) *noun* Predators are animals that hunt and kill other animals for food.

researcher (REE surch uhr) *noun* A researcher is a scientist who studies a given field of knowledge.

revered (rih VIHRD) *adjective* Something that is revered is loved, respected, or honored.

sacred (SAY krihd) *adjective* Something that is sacred is important to a people's beliefs.

scorpions (SKAWR pee uhnz) *noun* Scorpions are similar to spiders, with poison in their curved tails.

silkworms (SIHLK wurmz) *noun* Silkworms are caterpillars that produce fine threads of silk to make their cocoon. These caterpillars turn into moths.

smoker (SMOH kuhr) *noun* A smoker is a tool used by people who keep bees. It holds a small fire that makes smoke.

species (SPEE sheez) *noun* A species is a kind, sort, or class of plant or animal.

tarantulas (tuh RAN choo luhz) *noun* Tarantulas are large, hairy spiders. Their bite is painful.

thorax (THAWR aks) *noun* The thorax is the middle part of an insect's body, between the head and the abdomen.

traditional (truh DIHSH uh nuhl) *adjective* Traditional means same as or similar to earlier styles or customs.

trillion (TRIHL yehn) *adjective* A trillion insects can also be written as 1,000,000,000,000 insects.

wary (WEHR ee) *adjective* To be wary is to be on guard against something.

Web site (WEHB syt) *noun* A Web site is a group of pages on the Internet. You can see Web sites on a computer that is connected to the Internet.

whitefly (HWYT fly) *noun* A whitefly is a small insect with long wings. It often damages crops.

wrangler (RANG gluhr) *noun* A wrangler is a person who handles animals for a living.

Index